JAMES

a disciple of Jesus

© 1984 Rourke Publications, Inc.

Published by Geoffrey Butcher 1983

Published by Rourke Publications, Inc., P.O. Box 3328, Vero Beach, Florida 32964. Copyright © 1984 by Rourke Publications, Inc. All copyrights reserved. No part of this book may be reproduced in any form without written permission from the publisher. Printed in the United States of America.

Library of Congress Cataloging in Publication Data

Butcher, Geoffrey.
    James : a disciple of Jesus.

    (A Little Shepherd Book)
    Summary: Brief versions of miraculous events in the life of Jesus which James, one of the twelve apostles, witnessed.
    1. James, the Greater, Saint—Juvenile literature.
[1. Jesus Christ—Miracles.   2. James, the Greater, Saint.   3. Bible stories—N.T.]   I. Title.   II. Series.
BS2453.B88   1984   225.9'24   [B]   84-9848
ISBN 0-86625-252-5

JAMES

a disciple of Jesus

Written and illustrated by
GEOFFREY BUTCHER

Rourke Publications, Inc.
A Little Shepherd Book
Vero Beach, FL 32964

James and his brother John were fishermen.

When they were mending their nets one day Jesus came to them.

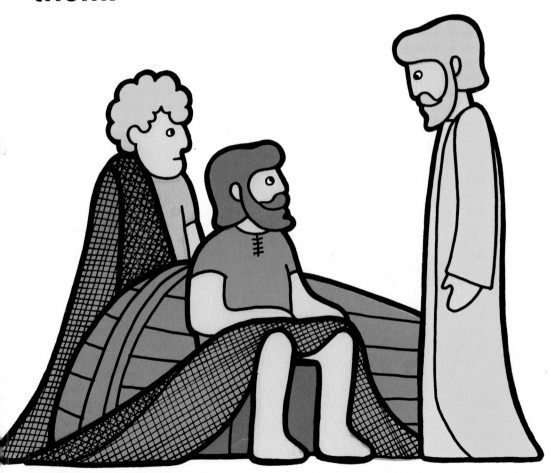

He asked them to leave their boats and nets and follow Him.

Soon James was one of the twelve special friends of Jesus.

They were James, John, Peter, Andrew, Philip, Bartholomew,

Matthew, Thomas, James son of Alphaeus, Simon, Thaddaeus and Judas.

James travelled with Jesus. He saw Jesus make blind people see again.

Jesus made lame people walk again and sick people well again.

Once when crossing a lake,
Jesus was asleep in the back
of the boat.

A terrible storm blew up.
Waves began to break over
the boat.

James and the others were afraid. They woke Jesus.

People there were crying, so Jesus sent them out of the room.

Jesus took James, John and Peter and went home with Jairus.

Jairus was asking Jesus for help when he heard that his daughter had died.

Jesus ordered the storm to stop and the wind and waves obeyed Him.

As James watched, Jesus took the girl's hand and she came to life again.

Wherever Jesus spoke many people came to listen to Him.

Once, Jesus wanted to feed many people who had followed Him for days.

The disciples had only seven loaves and a few small fishes.

Jesus thanked God for the food and the disciples shared it with the crowd.

When everyone had been fed there were seven baskets of scraps left over.

Jesus often took James, John and Peter away with Him.

One day Jesus took them up high to a mountain to pray.

There His face and clothes shone.
Moses and Elijah appeared at
His side.

A bright cloud came down and James and the others were afraid.

God's voice spoke, saying,
"This is my son whom I love.
Listen to Him!"

Later, Jesus told them to keep secret all they had seen. Soon He would die and rise from the dead.